Muse

First published in 2015 by
The Dedalus Press
13 Moyclare Road
Baldoyle
Dublin 13
Ireland

www.dedaluspress.com

Copyright © Gerry Murphy, 2015

ISBN 978 1 910251 05 8

All rights reserved.
No part of this publication may be reproduced in any form or by
any means without the prior permission of the publisher.

The moral right of the author has been asserted.

Dedalus Press titles are represented in the UK by
Central Books, 99 Wallis Road, London E9 5LN
and in North America by Syracuse University Press, Inc.,
621 Skytop Road, Suite 110, Syracuse, New York 13244.

Cover image, *Wo-mannequin Surprise Photo*,
copyright © Watermarkmrb | Dreamstime.com

The Dedalus Press receives financial assistance from
The Arts Council / An Chomhairle Ealaíon

Muse

Gerry Murphy

*To the Reverend Benny O'Neill,
with best wishes
Gerry Murphy
22nd April 2018.*

DEDALUS PRESS
DUBLIN, IRELAND

ACKNOWLEDGEMENTS

Thanks are due to the editors of the following publications where some of these poems, or versions of them, have previously appeared: *Poetry Ireland Review, The Stinging Fly, The SHOp, The Cork Literary Review, Cyphers, The Irish Times, The Glanmire Area News, Southword, Riddle Fence* and *Jeune Poésie d'Irlande*.

The author wishes to thank Patrick Crowley for his close reading of the manuscript of this book.

Contents

Muse / 11
The Other Half / 12
A Brief Romance / 13
Wallet Photograph / 15
Nausicaa / 16
Youth / 17
At Sixty / 18
Turn / 19
Close Call / 20
Train to Sligo / 21
Luminous Blue Nightie / 22
A Real Looker / 23
Romp / 24
The Corner House / 25
Genesis / 26
In Eden / 27
Paradise Lost / 28
Felix Culpa? / 29
Patriarch / 31
What Jesus Did Next / 32
According to Pindar / 34
Musing on Immortality / 35
Here We Go Again / 36
What Next? / 37
Bell's Field Reverie / 38
The Lyric Imperative / 39
Solace / 40
The Scribe / 41
Amongst Poets / 42
A Pact / 43
Why I Am A Poet / 44

A Trip to Fuente Grande / 45
Our Best Poets / 46
A Farewell to Neil Armstrong / 47
Spook / 48
Flashback / 49
Deus Ex Machina / 50
Tractor / 51
Dillon's Cross Wormhole / 52
Bud / 53
Chaos Theory / 54
Parallel Universe / 55
What's He Doing in There? / 56
Ceremony / 57
Goethe Arrives in Rome / 58
An Evening Out / 59
Let Daydreaming Composers Lie … / 60
De Profundis / 61
Astronomers / 62
"There'll be days like this…" / 63
A Little Nick / 64
Peace Process / 65
A Wet Evening in April / 66
Meditation / 67
Rescue / 68
Revenant / 69
The Boy Who Picked Up the Shilling
the Old Priest Dropped / 70
Self-Portrait on a Christmas Morning / 71
From Another Life / 72
On the Death of an Ex-Girlfriend / 73
Cortège / 74
The Well-Travelled Man / 75
Sailors / 76

Voyager

*To set out in sleep
for those distant galaxies
behind the eyelids.*

for Michaela Halvegård

Muse

I am writing naked
at the kitchen table
when you steal in
from the shower
and stand on tiptoe
at my shoulder.
A few drops from
your dripping hair
splash onto the lamp-lit page,
blurring the words
I am deploying in your honour.
With an abrupt kiss,
you slip into the bedroom,
your seal of approval
still tingling
from the nape of my neck
down into the small of my back
as I turn the dampened page
and begin again.

The Other Half

Not making love,
lying together
in an embrace
that may just be
the sweet spot
of all our embraces.
How did we get so *here?*
We dare not stir,
nor try to figure out
the tender mechanics
of how we stumbled
on this makeshift nirvana,
a single breathing entity.
But we do stir
and make love
and lose our place
and haven't found it since.

A Brief Romance

A flurry of snowflakes
swirls up
over the parapet
of Half Moon Bridge
and sweeps down
Capwell Road.
An empty taxi passes
along the South Douglas Road,
kicking up slush
and hooting
into the distance.
Inside my overcoat,
you are snuggling up
to my chest,
one kiss leading
to another.

In the kitchen,
a carefree chef
is preparing
his one and only speciality
as *All Blues* seeps in
from the bedroom,
where a bedside lamp
is picking out
the henna glints
in your glossy black hair,
while you read,
beautiful in glasses,
his odes to the daughters
of the lower-middle-classes.

The early evening sky
is dreaming you up:
between Sirius and Orion,
the exact blue-grey of your eyes.
The lighthouse is unfurling
the black Anarchist banner of your hair
over a flat, indifferent sea.
I am sitting, naked by the seismograph,
waiting for the warm aftershocks,
still numb from holding you.

I am in your arms,
locked in
the swaddling warmth
of your skin,
lulled by the drowsy beat
of your heart,
nuzzling your breasts
like a sleepy child,
wondering which beam
of morning light
will draw you out
and away again.

There was something
almost Zen-like
about the way
you didn't turn up that night.
I waited with extraordinary concentration
outside the appointed place,
long after the appointed hour,
trying to distinguish
the sound of the distant stars
from the cheerful hum
of passing traffic.

Wallet Photograph

Who will finally scrutinise
this long-cherished image:
a young woman
with a beautiful
but troubled face.
The disappointed mugger
tossing it in a ditch?
The indifferent rain
reducing it to pulp?
The crematorium assistant
snatching it from the flames?

Nausicaa

Not so much
an occasional feast,
as a regular ocular repast.
That photograph
on my bedside locker,
taken on the beach
at Tel Aviv
as you entered
your twenty-fourth year.
You are straddling
a deck-chair
in a black bikini,
a glint of mischief
in your eyes,
a gleam of light
at play in your
fabled dark hair.
Casually scanning the horizon
for shipwrecked mariners,
while clutching
a well-thumbed
copy of *Ulysses,*
cracked open
in your beautifully
tanned hands.

Youth

after Nazim Hikmet

So, here's the story:
for ten years
our hands haven't touched,
not to mention our lips.
I grow older here,
you wiser there.
Love of my life,
your neck is probably
a little more lined,
your breasts
a little less firm.
As for me,
I have an eight year start on you,
so keep a weather eye open
for the obituaries.
But surely, of all people,
we cannot possibly grow old.
We need another term
for ageing flesh,
for inevitable entropy.
Only those who have loved
no one but themselves
are doomed to grow old.

At Sixty

A heavy shower,
cold rain left over
from October,
whips back to bless
this May day.
I have already set sail
on the uncertain ocean
of ineluctable old age,
under the alternating flags
of intrigue and trepidation:
"to touch
the Happy Isles
and meet Achilles,
or wash down
with the gulfs".
I am trying hard
to be glum
but it's impossible.
I've just been kissed,
kissed by Oonagh Montague.

Turn

for Kay

You come out
onto the balcony,
out of the hubbub
of full, contented tables
to take a phone call.
A day like any other,
a quotidian dullness
seeping into your bones,
your soul squeezed down
into your shoes.
Then, as you make
a half-turn to go back
into the restaurant,
a rare gleam of sunlight,
angling through the rooftop louvres,
snags in your still blonde hair
and suddenly you're eighteen
all over again.

Close Call

I don't know what you were thinking
(actually I do)
pushing me into that doorway,
kissing me into a breathless ferment
and then almost erasing me,
limb by shuddering limb,
with your frenzied frottage.
We were on the way
to the railway station,
you to meet your boyfriend
from the late train,
I to break off long before
and make my way home
without a hint of affection.
Perhaps his train was early,
or, more likely,
we had been kissing too long
and too well,
because when we emerged,
flushed, mussed-up and panting
from that feral maul,
he was all but upon us.
I strode on,
dishevelled but purposeful,
towards the station,
you drew him into
your still trembling arms.

Train to Sligo

I remember the lush
summer landscape
unfurling at a lick
across the window
and the clickety-click
rhythm of the train
transmitting its insistent signal
straight to my groin
and then you,
snuggled up to me on the seat,
wearing that cut-away T-shirt
which allowed the occasional
glimpse of your breasts
(oh those pert kissable breasts)
and that twitching erection straining
against the zipper of my jeans
and my futile attempts
to reverse its tumescence
with a whispered decade of the Rosary,
when I had only to look across the carriage
to the pair of nuns who were staring at us
with monumental disapproval from their
quivering mounds of rectitude.

Luminous Blue Nightie

After a few days of the dry heaves
the cat coughs up the space-station
seemingly undamaged in a sticky fur-ball
the moon ferry's engines switch from
a worrying rattle to a smooth reassuring hum
the Earth splits open right on schedule
the stars glitter closer and closer brighter
and brighter my girlfriends suddenly apologise.

They're dragging the river for yet another
homeless victim beaten to death by off-duty
Samaritans ragged-winged seraphim are being
hooked and hauled down to orbit the lighthouse
a massive whirlpool of grease is on the move from
the Persian Gulf out into the Indian Ocean the *last*
Last Mohican is opening the first Multiplex on the moon.

It's all right for you Wonder Woman
seven feet seven inches of ineffable beauty
in a luminous blue nightie leading a pair
of identical leopards around a lake's shimmering
edge in moonlight I'm still working on that
elusive one-hour erection (ten-minute orgasms)
with manuals creams abrasives bull's blood
yogic breathing liquid suspension open heart
manipulation blow-up dolls bi-location and
signed editions of the lives of the saints.

That midnight phone-fuck is keeping me awake
a ten-second jerk-off I thought I'd have forgotten
by now but that's love for you.

A Real Looker

after Rumi

Has anyone seen that woman
who used to come round here?
High cheek-boned and beautiful,
quick to laughter,
just as quick to seriousness
and fixing the already broken world.

Has anyone heard of her?
The whole of Egypt
nearly went to ruin once
for such beauty.
I'd gladly travel the globe
for word of her,
even second or third-hand.

Come to think of it, I have.

Romp

i.m. Sergei Esenin

After sharing the last can of beer,
we emerged from the kitchen
into the wreckage of another wild student party.
The marijuana was smoked,
except for a few flecks
we managed to retrieve from the carpet.
We burnt these on a spoon,
ate the ashes and went mad.
We rustled up some white paint
and a couple of sponges from the garage
and set out on our mission.
We started with the usual slogans:
"Smash The State" on our own back gate,
"Property Is Theft" two doors down,
"All Power To The Proletariat"
on the surgery door
and "Kill The Collaborating Poor"
on the corner shop window.
As we approached the University
we entered our religious phase:
"God Is Dead And So Is St. Peter"
on the black hoarding outside the main gates,
"Strangle The Druids With Their Own Entrails"
on the Chaplain's Notice Board
and finally, our *pièce de résistance*,
all along the steep convent wall
in three-feet-high letters:
"Here At Night The Nuns Take Down Christ's
Trousers".

The Corner House

after Abu Nuwas

One night I took a few old friends,
demons for drink, to my local.
It was so late even God was in bed
but the landlord woke
to my insistent knocking.
At first he was reluctant to open
but when I pleaded with him,
using every noble name
on the better side of his family,
he relented.
Even the door seemed to enjoy opening
the way he did it.
"Come in, boys, and welcome,
the later the safer as the man said."
"The night's gone out of it," I replied
"but home and dry we'll wet our whistle."
And we settled in until dawn.

for Fearghal MacGabhann

Genesis

for John F. Deane

In the beginning
was Heaven and Earth.
And the Earth
was void and empty
and darkness was upon
the face of the deep.
And the Spirit of God
moved over the waters.
And God said:
"Let there be Fred Astaire,"
and there was Fred Astaire.
And God said:
"Whoops! Light, let there be light?
Sorry Fred, getting ahead of Myself."

In Eden

for Paul Bensimon

Adam in Eden,
Adam running all day in Eden,
Adam running through the forests in Eden,
Adam running beside the rivers in Eden,
beside the Pison and the lands of Havilah,
beside the Gihon and whole of Ethiopia,
beside the Hiddekel and vast Assyria,
running beside the mighty Euphrates itself in Eden.
Adam running in Eden,
Adam running effortlessy, running without rest,
running without hunger or thirst in Eden.
Adam running, running, running in Eden.
Adam running long before Eve in Eden.

Paradise Lost

after Milton

The black cormorant
squatting in the Tree of Life
plots our giddy Fall.

Felix Culpa?

Already in Eden (just walk up the Euphrates) there was confusion you would think that after taking the trouble of creating Adam and subsequently Eve God would have kept them out of harm's way at least until they could get their bearings especially since he neglected to endow them with any great sense of awareness and crucially little or no self-awareness which left them understandably helpless before the wiles of the Serpent (how did he get in? how did someone only recently in revolt against and hurled from the shimmering vault of Heaven to the burning marl of Hell seem to have the full run of Paradise?) incidentally were Adam and Eve really our first parents or the first we hear about in any detail were they ostensibly just another in a long line of botched experiments or were they actually created to lure the Serpent out into the open again after a gloomy aeon licking his bruises and nursing his devastated pride to see if he could be provoked into another grand assault on the Citadel of Heaven if only for the amusement of its chronically bored inhabitants and another thing what happened to those people mentioned earlier in Genesis who were reportedly made in the image and likeness of God and just as suddenly disappear from the text and what about Lillith? where does she fit in? not a word apart from the mythopoeic legends anyway God forbids Adam and Eve on pain of death to eat from the Tree of Knowledge knowing full well that they will and sure enough after listening to the promptings of the Serpent Eve bites into the apple and quickly persuades Adam to follow suit although without the Serpent they probably would have gotten around to eating the forbidden fruit eventually you can only eat so much from the Tree of Life before you start craving something different still it makes you wonder what would have happened if Adam had refused the proffered fruit (no thanks, love, I'm stuffed, I just ate a Unicorn) would Eve now intellectually awakened have stayed in Paradise with the holy fool or taken her chances with the Serpent? would God have created a second companion for Adam? (hey, go easy on the ribs) so with the expulsion from Eden the whole nine yards begins to unfold a kind of Big Bang in slow-motion if you will by the by it seems the first couple were blissfully unaware of the sexual possibilities of their new situation was it a case of some highly embarrassed Archangel handing them a few manuals and creams as they trudged out through the Gates of Paradise?

Patriarch

Imagine
an eight-year-old atheist
kicking his father
on the shins
while disputing
the dubious veracity
of the Old Testament.

Now imagine the father's name
is Joseph.

What Jesus Did Next

Which brings me to Lazarus you know the one I mean now a certain man was sick named Lazarus none other than the brother of Martha and Mary very close friends of Jesus and in whose company he seemed most at ease well anyway Jesus learns that Lazarus is sick and you think drop everything and off to Bethany but no Jesus maintains that this sickness is not unto death so on with the tour even including Judea where threats were made against his life and people would have been only too willing to hand him over to the High Priest for investigation anyway Jesus speaks about Lazarus again our friend Lazarus sleepeth but I go that I may wake him out of sleep so you're thinking back to Bethany but no Jesus lingers in Judea and then announces Lazarus is dead and I am glad for your sakes I was not there to the intent you may believe nevertheless let us go to him now then up steps me bold Thomas and says he let us also go that we may die with him and you're thinking speak for yourself Didymus I didn't sign up for this loaves and fishes yes but death that's a bit much anyway it's off to Bethany at long last only to find Lazarus is already four days in the tomb so you think that's that but no Jesus speaks in his usual riddling way with Mary and Martha when they insist that had Jesus been present their brother would not have died to which he replies that since he is both the resurrection and the life then if they but believe in him their brother shall live somewhere around here Jesus seems to have decided to bring Lazarus back to life not that anyone in Bethany was thinking in those terms especially the sisters who spoke of meeting their brother in Paradise it is also possible that Jesus had made up his mind to raise Lazarus as soon as he learned of his illness maybe even long before who knows what timescale he was working on he may have been planning a spectacular for months which would explain his lack of urgency when he received the news of Lazarus' illness and his cryptic remarks to his disciples not to mention all those references to his state of mind at the time I mean of course he groaned in spirit and was troubled and Jesus again groaning in himself and the famous Jesus wept he seemed uncomfortable with the constant clamouring for miracles and as for the grim procession of the blind the halt and the lame not to mention a veritable slew of lepers surrounding him at every opportunity this is not what he was about his mantra was profoundly simple my kingdom is not of this world not that too many took much notice after all his first miracle was all but dragged out of him by his own mother somewhere along the way he may have decided all right they want miracles I'll give them miracles except that on this occasion he was among his closest friends not at all the type to insist on the extraordinary his presence in their grieving was enough and they were actually aghast when he asked for the tomb to be opened saying Lord he hath been dead four days he stinketh just there you think just there he should have let it go …

According to Pindar

for Roisín & Deirdre

Eventually, even Asclepius
went in over his head,
frazzled to ashes by Zeus
for daring to bring back the dead.

Musing on Immortality

for Billy Ramsell

No, not that appalling half-life
envisaged by Plato: "unable to chew or sip"
amongst the ideal archetypes of his gloomy Elysium,
nor condemned to swarm with those twittering shades,
blown from one end of Hades to the other
by searing, contrary winds,
or, worse still, to be faffing about on fluffy white wings,
cloud-hopping from one angelic chorus to the next
in an otherwise abandoned Paradise.
I mean the vibrant, here-and-now existence
of the old Greek Gods,
the ability to act, to intervene, to influence.
To enter the fray at its most intense
and suffer its bone-shuddering clash,
secure in the knowledge
that you were impervious to harm.
To have the full run of Heaven and Earth,
indulging your every whim instantly,
from breakfast-rolls to houris,
complete body-shaves to interminable blow jobs.
To spend a thousand years writing a haiku,
a thousand years googling yourself,
a thousand years rummaging through
old photographs of ex-girlfriends,
without any appreciable sense of wasted time.
Best of all, to choose some idyllic moments
from each of those shining sagas,
freeze-frame them and expand them into infinity,
before dwelling, briefly or at length,
within their sweet, eternal amber.
Hold that thought, here's my quarter pounder!

Here We Go Again

So, what would you like to return as
in your next lie?
asked the Angel of Death
as she pulled me out from under the juggernaut
and peeled me gingerly from my bike.
Oh, I thought reincarnation was the Hindu Department,
I replied.
Well, yes but Himself wants to give it a go,
Heaven is getting crowded and the longest dwellers
are complaining that most newcomers just want
to watch Champion's League highlights continually,
so it's on the menu for a while.
As I was saying, your next life?
she continued,
pointing out that the current choice of incarnation
was between Novelist and Short Story Writer.
That's a choice? I gasped.
Afraid so, himself has a thing about everyone
taking a turn at the bottom of the slush pile,
building character and all that.
What if I refuse both? I ventured.
Then it's oblivion for a millennium
and back to the very same choice.
Fuck!
Fuck indeed.
Look, I need a decision now, she said, somewhat sharply.
You're sure I'm dead, not just winded?

What Next?

for Conal Creedon

On Devonshire Street,
the brilliant moonlight
is angling through a gap
in the chimney field,
to briefly illumine
the brass number plate
on your front door.
A man is reading a faded
planning notice on the boarded-up
windows of the Inchigeela Dairy.
In the nearby Funeral Home,
the undertaker's apprentice
is practising his graveside manner
on the corpse of a pharmacist.

Between your side gate
and the gate of the old Munster Hotel,
ghost teams are playing soccer.

Bell's Field Reverie

Can you imagine
the wall at the top of Bell's Field
as the ramparts of the Alhambra?
Gurranabraher as the Abaicin?
Knocknaheeny as Sacre Monte?
Yet on an October afternoon
with a westering sun
picking out small shiny surfaces
to glint off as it sinks.
With Shandon's tower
and the turrets of St. Vincents
in perfect silhouette
on their respective heights.
With the hooting of distant traffic,
the faint cries of homebound schoolchildren,
the convent bell three minutes early,
the Cathedral peal three minutes late.
With the Lee's majestic sweep past the Maltings,
almost imitating the gilded pomp of the Genil,
can you picture Cork briefly putting on
the timeless grandeur of Granada?

Neither can I.

The Lyric Imperative

for Tomás Ó Canainn

An end-of-the-world wind
is buffeting the woods
along the Glashaboy River.
The trees are in turmoil,
straining against the earth,
as if to pull up their roots
and scramble over the hill
out of the swirling uproar.
As they once upped sticks
and followed Orpheus,
drawn by his bewitching songs,
his disconcerting lyre.

Solace

after Milosz

I praise brother pen
as he puts forth twigs and leaves
and such bitter fruit.

The Scribe

after the Irish, 9th century

An oak tree shelters me,
a blackbird frets in its branches.
Across my open notebook,
flickers of sunlight
at play through the leaves.

for Clíona Ní Ríordáin

Amongst Poets

after Rubén Darío

The Muse walks by our table a trifle piqued,
someone finds the exact, wounding phrase.
A line of poetry flares up and dies away,
a whiff of brimstone floating in its wake.

A Pact

after Ezra Pound

I make a pact with you, Orpheus,
I have resisted you long enough.
I come to you as a grown man
who has enjoyed a long childhood.
It was you who cut the new wood,
it is for us to carve it.
We have one sap and one root,
let there be traffic between us.

Why I Am A Poet

Is it all down to my father's habit
of smoking Sweet Afton cigarettes
and my reading and re-reading
Burns' lovely couplet on the packet:
"Flow gently sweet Afton amang thy green braes,
flow gently I'll sing thee a song in thy praise."
Was it my uncle Paddy soaring
on those kite-like tropes of Omar Khayyám
between gulps of mulled porter?
Or my mother, squirreling away
those hurriedly scribbled notes
beneath the sofa cushions,
which I would often find
but could never quite get,
verses from her own lost Rubáiyát?

A Trip to Fuente Grande

Forgive my cheerfulness, Federico,
I am on my way back from Viznar
to Granada under the influence
of that sudden lift in spirits
which often follows a visit to a grave.
I am whistling "McNamara's Band"
as I saunter back, forgoing the bus.
The Colonia (where you spent your last night)
has been demolished
and only a few scattered mill-stones
give any clue to its former use.
The Memorial Park (where you died)
is situated half-way between
Viznar and Fuente Grande,
as if both wished to share in the honour,
but more likely that neither
wants the implicit blame of its presence.
It sits in well-tended isolation,
in the pine-covered hills,
giddy with poetry.

Our Best Poets

after Merton

While the Universe continues
its helpless outward drift
towards ultimate dissolution –
the *Unmoved Mover* dozing at the wheel –
while the *Zeitgeist* insists on pessimism,
despair, madness and annihilation,
our best poets are running wild
through the moonlit graveyards of Literature,
desecrating the lichen-covered monuments
of the long-forgotten dead.

A Farewell to Neil Armstrong

Somewhere,
out beyond Orion,
a steadily degrading broadcast
of the 1969 Moon landing
is playing to the indifferent Void:
"That's one small step for a man,
one giant leap for mankind that's
one small step for a man
on gian leap for mankin
that on sma ste fo a ma
o gia lea f manki
tha o sm st f m o gi
le mank th s s r o gi
le f man
t g l ma
m m m
m m
m …

Spook

Aslant
of all known airways,
she passes high, spectral, white.
Displaying no contrail, utterly silent,
a ghost-machine in perpetual flight.

Flashback

after Paul Jeffcott

He's done this before,
a series of rolls, side-slips and spirals
at Mach 3 and pulled out safely,
but this is new.
He seems to be shrinking in his seat,
his helmet swinging loose,
his flight-suit already
six sizes too big
as he warps back rapidly
through youth, teenage and childhood,
until he's a baby
waving his tiny arms and wailing
in the cockpit of a plummeting F-16.

Deus Ex Machina

after Derek Mahon

What monstrous intervention
explains this enormous gearbox
rusting in the forest?

Tractor

after Karen Solie

Bigger than a barn and twice as long:
the Buhler Versatile 2360.
Possessed of the ecology
of a small tropical island,
part heat, part cloud, part dust,
it emerges full-blown, turbo-cooled
and ready for action from our deepest needs.
What used to take the 2359 a week,
it handles in a day and on a quarter of the fuel.
At seven hundred and fifty thousand dollars,
we hope to own it outright by 2023.

Dillon's Cross Wormhole

The yawning man
is waving at me as he drives past.
He is yawning so widely
I cannot recognise him.
He is yawning so deeply
it seems as if he will swallow
his passengers, his van,
the junction, the street,
the city, the country,
the continent, the planet,
the galaxy, the Universe
and himself.

Bud

for Karen Solie

It starts
from a flawed infinity,
particles flying apart
at the speed of light,
fractals branching and branching
(now a Cathedral, now a railway station)
until a fighter jet, in black livery,
hangs from the Tree of Chaos
like unwelcome fruit.

Chaos Theory

At the hint of rain,
the old lady
pops open her umbrella,
making her startled companion
jump from the pavement
into the path of a swiftly
approaching juggernaut,
which, swerving to avoid him,
flattens a cyclist
full-length into the tarmac,
launches a baby-stroller (baby included)
through the window
of a derelict bookshop
and shreds the wings
of a passing Amazonian butterfly.

Parallel Universe

for Tony Sheehan

We were cycling
along a quiet sunlit road,
between Leamlara and Lisgoold
that lazy Summer afternoon.
Burdened with tired legs
and an ever-growing thirst,
we laboured on manfully
until we spotted a shop up ahead,
a green-painted, corrugated structure,
topped by a whitewashed roof.
We stopped, dismounted and entered
its neat, gleaming interior,
with its rows of sweet jars, throbbing fridge,
obscure agricultural products
and glossy farming journals.
We bought two cans of Coke
from the timid but courteous girl
behind the counter and after a little
light banter about city cyclists
getting lost in the vast countryside,
cycled on into that glorious day.
A few weeks later
I was retracing our journey
and stopped at the same shop,
only to find it closed.
I peered through the grimy windows
to discover the roof fallen-in, a derelict interior
and mice tracks trailing hither and thither
through the accumulated dust of years.

What's He Doing in There?

He's found a portal to the nearest star
in the wardrobe and he's ferrying
highly unstable Dark Matter
across the Milky Way every night
in his dead mother's handbag,
he's hopping around the bedroom
saying the Rosary.
He's re-enacting the last five minutes
of the All Ireland Hurling Final of 1952
with a broken chair leg and a rolled-up sock
to his own whispered commentary,
he's dropping his left shoe
and placing his right shoe softly on the floor.
He's building a Particle Accelerator
in an old hat-box with which he intends
to mimic the conditions immediately before
or immediately after the Big Bang,
he's cooking a moose.
He's repairing a small tear
in the Space-Time Continuum
before it gets any bigger and threatens
the continuing existence of the Universe,
he's trimming his toenails.
He's constructing an Ark out of broken furniture,
following the precise Biblical dimensions.
So far he has a stray cat, a dead hamster
and a mange-ridden dog scratching around
in its massive hold.
He's wondering what I'm doing in here.

Ceremony

after Guémar

We waited,
hour after hour dissolving
in the afternoon drizzle.
When he arrived
everyone snapped to attention,
even the dozing curate.
The President
didn't even glance at us,
he stared out past us
at the brooding sea,
absent-mindedly
scratching his crotch.

Goethe Arrives in Rome

Approaching nearer and nearer
to the centre of Romanism,
surrounded on all sides by Catholics,
boxed-up in a sedan
with a blabbering priest,
I cannot shake the nagging conviction
that all traces of original Christianity
are here utterly extinct.

An Evening Out

after Berlioz

One evening,
we went to explore
the Baths of Caracalla together.
As we traversed the impressive ruins,
we were debating the question
of merit and demerit in human behaviour
and its reward in this life
rather than the next.
While I was, as usual,
propounding an outrageous thesis
in opposition to Mendelssohn's
strictly orthodox view,
he slipped and tumbled down
a flight of steep, eroded steps.
As he was lying in a heap
at the bottom, battered and bruised,
I couldn't help remarking:
"Look at that for Divine justice,
I blaspheme, you fall."

Let Daydreaming Composers Lie ...

for John Gibson

Here's the young Verdi,
an altar boy daydreaming
in his local church.
Caught up in the music of the ceremony
and the busy frescos on the ceiling,
he is deaf to the priest's repeated request for water.
The priest gives him a clout to the head
and knocks him down the altar steps,
leaving him dazed and confused.
When he recovers he solemnly declares
that the priest who struck him
will be struck down in his turn
by God himself.
Some years later the priest is praying
in a church in another parish,
when it is struck by lightning
and he is killed stone dead.

De Profundis

after Arrigo Boito

Here's Mephistopheles
leaving the nethermost
depths of Hell,
clinging to the back
of a bat-winged demon,
hurrying up
through the circles
like a floater
in the eye
of a feverish girl.

Astronomers

after Zbigniew Herbert

Drunkards
drink down to the bottom
in one quick draft.
But seeing their grim reflections
in the dregs, they shudder.
Through the glass
of the empty bottle,
they observe hazy, faraway worlds.
If they had clearer heads
and better taste,
they would be astronomers.

"There'll be days like this…"

A rustle of sharpshooters
on the roof of the Cathedral,
Spring about its business
in the Square below.
On a park bench,
near the fountain,
lulled by water gossip,
light falls aslant
on the drowsing terrorist.

A Little Nick

He cut his left index finger
opening a tin of beans last night.
It still smarts this morning
but thankfully the bleeding has stopped.
He will remove the plaster
before he leaves the house.
Somehow it wouldn't look right,
it could be misinterpreted,
or, at the very least, over-emphasised;
it would certainly be considered significant.
He knows exactly what he has to do:
walk briskly into the restaurant
and press the detonator,
walk briskly into the restaurant
and press the detonator …

Peace Process

A charming English couple
have asked me to take their photo
on the steps of Shandon Steeple.
I readily oblige,
but only as I snap them
do I notice the 'Brits Out' graffito,
neatly dividing their grinning heads.

A Wet Evening in April

after Kavanagh

The birds sang in the wet trees
and as I listened to them it was a hundred years from now
and I was dead and someone else listened to them,
thinking of someone else again listening to them
a hundred years from then.

Meditation

Across the river,
a young ash tree
coming late into leaf
after a long Winter,
blesses all it surveys.
Directly in front,
protruding from the bank,
a cannon from the Crimean War,
aimed with uncanny precision
at my window.
If it could speak,
its eloquent retort
would concentrate
my scattered strivings
towards Nirvana.

Rescue

Woken from a face-down,
half-smothered-in-the-pillow sleep
by a luminous mandala
unfolding behind my eyes.
It may have flared up on the brink
of some significant threshold,
or been triggered
by a lack of oxygen,
but was now printing itself
on every available surface
in the bedroom.
Quickly expanding from its centre,
busy with molten radiance,
out to its intricate, geometric edges,
before gradually fading
back into the teeming unconscious,
leaving me blessed,
perplexed and breathless.

Revenant

Already on the stairs,
I turn back to check
that I have secured
the attic door,
when I am
face-to-face with him.
Not six feet away,
the ghost of some
previous tenant,
staring at me frankly,
with a hint
of a smile just faded,
or just about to break
on his lips.

The Boy Who Picked Up the Shilling the Old Priest Dropped

He is running wild
hugging the planet's steep curve
down to the sweet shop.

Self-Portrait on a Christmas Morning

The boy goes patter-pat
down the chilly stairs,
his six-year-old heart
thumping in his chest.
Agog to discover
if Santa has left
that hoped-for gift
beneath the tree.
To find a cold bare parlour,
a childless old man
staring back at him
from the hallway mirror,
a clock ticking loudly
through the empty house.

From Another Life

You wake,
to a tiny shoe-print
on the skylight glass.
As if a baby
had been toddling
across the rooftops
during the night,
or watching you sleep.

On the Death of an Ex-Girlfriend

i.m. Marian Crowley

In the pantheon of ex-girlfriends
you hold an honoured place.
If not my first ever,
then in the first rank
of my ex-girlfriends.
A most kissable mouth
in a most kissable face.
Not that you allowed
much kissing.
We did not see eye to eye
on religion or politics or sex,
or anything else for that matter.
I was struggling through
my young anarchist phase
(giddily quoting Bakunin to your aghast mother:
"the last king strangled in the guts of the last priest…")
while you rose in the ranks
of the Legion of Mary.
Rose too high eventually
into that forbidding ether
for us ever again
to find common ground,

comrade beloved.

Cortège

for Matthew Sweeney

Somewhere,
back at the traffic lights perhaps,
the chief mourning cars
may have lost contact
with the hearse –
and then caught up again,
only to find
the ice-cream van
clipping along cheerfully
behind the coffin.

Either that,
or the ice-cream man is dead.

The Well-Travelled Man

after Leonidas of Tarentum

With courage, when that day comes,
seek the kingdom of the dead.
The way lies before you,
simple to find, easy to tread.
Neither steep nor narrow,
but broad, straight and true.
And sloping gently downhill
all the way to Pluto
and his grimly cheerful crew.

for Liam 'Tubs' McCarthy

Sailors

after Neruda

At sea for all of our storm-tossed lives,
we sail at last into some tranquil port,
where Death greets us, dressed as an Admiral.